# DESTINATION MASTERY

## 7 Steps to Viral Success

By: Ruben West

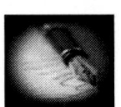

BSI Publishing House
www.businesssavvyinc.com

**Copyright © 2014 R. West Enterprises, LLC, All rights reserved**

No part of this publication may be excerpted, reproduced, transmitted in any form or by any means electronic or mechanical, photocopied, or scanned except as permitted under 107 or 108 of the 1976 United States Copyright Act, or printed for distribution or resale without express written permission from the author.

Published by BSI Publishing House, P.O. Box 461, Grand Blanc, MI 48480. Cover Design by BSI Design Studio.

Edited by Mia Zachary

Printed in the United States of America

ISBN: 978-1-312-47073-6

Dedication

This book is dedicated to my children Monica, Spencer, and Robinson, my wife Robin, my parents Robert and Rosetta, as well as the rest of my family and friends that continue to encourage me. Thank you for your love and support. Never stop pursuing your dreams. To Edwina Blackman, RN; Thank you for speaking life and truth in to me at a time when I needed it most. I listened.

# TABLE OF CONTENTS

| | | |
|---|---|---|
| **Author's Note** | | i |
| **Introduction** | | 1 |
| **Step One:** | Directing Your Thoughts | 13 |
| | Action Items: Overcoming Self-doubt | 29 |
| **Step Two:** | Acting with Gratitude & Faith | 33 |
| | Action Items: Increasing Gratitude & Faith | 45 |
| **Step Three:** | Choosing the Right Associations | 49 |
| | Action Items: Creating Your Dream Team | 63 |
| **Step Four:** | Sacrificing for What Is Necessary | 67 |
| | Action Items: Sacrificing for Success | 83 |
| **Step Five:** | Embracing the Idea of Failure | 87 |
| | Action Items: Overcoming Setbacks | 101 |
| **Step Six:** | Having the Will to Succeed | 105 |
| | Action Items: Taking Command & Control | 123 |
| **Step Seven:** | Redefining Your Authentic Self | 127 |
| | Action Items: Living Without Regrets | 139 |
| **Conclusion** | Working with Mentors & Coaches | 143 |
| | Action Items: What You Really Want | 149 |
| **Afterword** | | 157 |

# AUTHOR'S NOTE

The # symbol has taken on great popularity lately in the social media world. It is simply, a way for people to search Twitter, Facebook, and other social media sites for the words following the # symbol. At points throughout the book, you will find key words and phrases that have been "hashtagged". I welcome you to share these words of wisdom on your social media sites and let others know how this book has affected your life. Share the hashtag and tag @RubenWest. Let your friends know how this book can change their lives, as well!

At the end of each chapter, I've included some Action Items. The tendency to skim over the action items is normal. However, I want you to play *full out*. Even if you question whether you need to do this exercise or not; please do it anyway. Writing things down is a direct step towards the mastery process. Look at it this way. What gets written gets measured. What gets measured gets monitored. What gets monitored gets mastered. In addition to being able to reach a level of mastery, completing the action steps can also help you to uncover and discover emotions that are hidden below the surface.

I have also included Mastery Tips after each section. These tips are a quick powerful narrative to give you motivation and inspiration while you put in the perspiration along your journey. Feel free to share these tips on your social media pages. Just be sure to let everyone know that you got them *from Destination Mastery,* by Ruben West. Enjoy!

# INTRODUCTION
## Defining the Viral Success System

*"Destiny is no matter of chance. It is a matter of choice. It is not a thing to be waited for; it is a thing to be achieved."* — William Jennings Bryan

Who are you? You are yourself. But what is self? What does 'self' mean? From a biologic aspect, self is what is currently in the body. Anything different introduced into the body is considered 'non-self' or foreign. The self-aspect of the body then recognizes these different organisms as foreign and launches an attack against them, surrounding them and destroying them. This is the body's natural way of defending it's 'self'. In medicine, we call this process immunology.

But how can this same theory apply to our mindset? When we think of our 'self' from a mindset standpoint, we can describe it as our current set of beliefs, our habits, and all the events and influences that have shaped us to be who we are today. It is our beliefs about ourselves that shapes our mindset. These beliefs may have been developed at a very early age, either from the influences of our parents, our peer groups, or things we saw or heard. All of this together caused us to develop a certain set of beliefs about who we are and where we 'fit in'.

So how are the biologic definition of 'self' and the mindset explanation of 'self' related? Take a look at this example: Imagine feeling like something is wrong with your body. You go to your doctor and, after a series of tests and a period of uncertainty; you get the news that you need a transplant. You start thinking about the many ways your life is about to change. The uncertainty almost paralyzes you, but you realize that you must act for your life's sake.

Good news! Everything goes well as far as your donor matching, your surgical procedure, and your initial recovery. However, shortly after this vital transplant procedure, your body starts to reject the new organ. Wait, what? Even though it was exactly what you needed? Even though this was the best possible option for you? Yes.

Why does this happen? Let me explain. Imagine feeling like something is wrong in your mind;

that something about you or within you needs to undergo a change. It might be a need or desire like:
- Weight loss or a need to exercise
- A new career or advancement in your current job
- Additional training or education
- A new business venture or entrepreneurship
- A new relationship, or friendship
- Better habits for saving, spending, organizing, and/or cleaning.

Then you take your newfound enlightenment to the next level with some preliminary actions. These are usually emotionally driven tasks that give you an immediate sense of accomplishment. You did something like:
- Buying new workout clothes or joining a gym
- Looking at training and educational classes
- Cleaning out your car, closet or basement
- Getting a new calendar or planner for better organization; And, especially, purchasing motivational books, CD, or DVD

Over the next days, you feel great, you look great and you're excited. Hey, you're changing! You're altering your life course! You're going to feel better about yourself, your life and your outlook. Over the next weeks, though, you might start to struggle. You feel fantastic one day, but frustrated or even defeated the next. Wait, something inside of you asks, "You want to change"

What's going on? Your Viral Success System (V.S.S.) works in much the same way as your body's actual immune system. The mission of your V.S.S. is to destroy that foreign invader, right? Well, in this case, the "enemy assault" comes typically from new ideas or new thought processes like those suggested in personal development.

Although the changes you tried to make are needed and necessary, your V.S.S. usually rejects them shortly after implementation, much like the body might reject a new transplant organ. But, why? Why would your body reject something that you so desperately want and need?

The most important process that takes place in your body is stasis. Stasis refers to a state of balance and stability; a condition in which things do not change, move, or progress. The V.S.S. blocks out or attacks foreign invaders (new thoughts or ideas) from your mind in order to help guide your actions, maintain stasis and protect the "self".

The biological need for stasis is exactly why, psychologically, you often achieve only short term success with the positive changes you try to make in your lives. The Viral Success System breaks down as follows:

- Your sustained thoughts create your mindset
- Mindset drives your words and actions
- Your words and actions are seen as "self"
- "Self" gets protected and defended by the V.S.S.
- New thought processes are attacked as "non-self"

#ChangeDoesntHappenOvernight and neither did your V.S.S. It's important to recognize that the development of your V.S.S. has been a life-long process. Throughout your life, you get instructions and information from a variety of sources. Parents spend years teaching you, trying to instill in you both a concept of right and wrong, and encourage you towards the road to success.

Some of those lessons are very deliberately planned. Interestingly, many of these lessons are not so deliberate or even intentional. For example, when a parent says one thing, yet does another. These actions would send mixed signals to any child. This form of ambiguity could emerge negatively at a later point in time. This can create a toxic mindset leading to a negative self-image. This self-image then gets defended by the V.S.S., making change seem impossible.

The school years are a time when your V.S.S. is vulnerable. This is when ideas of self-worth, self-image, attraction and attractiveness, intelligence, plus the propensity for success all begin to take root. You can be exposed to ideas and thoughts that aren't so positive, tainting your spirits and cementing a negative self-image.

Teachers, counselors, and educators program messages in a student's V.S.S. every day that you are in class. Just as with parents, there are times when you are programming information that was never intended. Unfortunately, most teachers don't have the luxury of time to listen to the hopes, dreams, and aspirations of each and every student they encounter. Therefore, they offer few words of encouragement, not realizing that they could actually be discouraging the student from their life's mission.

Once an individual has affixed limitations for success in their mind, it is seen as "self" and these limiting beliefs are now defended by your V.S.S.

Have you ever had someone tell you that they didn't think you would be successful? Or that they didn't think you would amount to anything? This is exactly what happens to many young minds on a daily basis. Imagine being a fly on the wall in a 5$^{th}$ grade classroom and seeing all the kids at their desks ready to start the day. You hear the teacher say, "get your paper and pencil out and get ready and write down these vocabulary words."

You see all the kids act with swiftness except one, who is a little bit reluctant. He knows what is coming. Now you watch as Mrs. Edwards, a tall, older, no-nonsense teacher's assistant, approach this young student. "Get your paper and pencil out." She says.

Reluctantly, this child let out a sigh of frustration. He'd been down this road before. As he began to write the words, Mrs. Edwards spoke in his ear. "Why is that pencil in your left hand again? I thought you were working on becoming right handed." "I've tried, but it's not working," he replied repulsed by the usual smell of coffee and cigarettes on her breath. "That's the problem," she said. "You're a quitter. You'll never amount to anything."

I was that young 5th grade boy! Mrs. Edwards felt there was no use in this world for left-handedness. She said that if I was ever going to amount to anything, I had to change. I tried and tried, time and time again. However, my V.S.S. had recorded every word Mrs. Edwards spoke and every feeling I had when she did. I believed it was impossible for me to switch.

Has someone tried to make you become

someone you're not? Or maybe they wanted you to change because there was something they didn't like about you? (In a way, this is like a large-scale, societal V.S.S. When people see you as "other", rather than like "self", they decide to dislike something about you and want you to change.) These judgments can lead to long-term, deep-seeded issues. They can cause long-term negative issues that often go undetected.

In his book, *Psycho-Cybernetics*, Dr. Maxwell Moltz discusses the three factors that can lead to information being imprinted on the subconscious mind.
1) The statement is being made by an authority figure,
2) The statement or underlying message is often repeated,
3) The statement is made with force or emotion.

Mrs. Edwards was definitely an authority figure and I heard her chastise me so often that I believed her words. Whether it was Mrs. Edwards' intention or not, her words were received as forceful and harsh.

Because all three factors were present, you can easily see the negative effect of having an educator come in, day after day, and tell you that because you can't switch from being left-handed to right-handed, you'll never have a place in this world nor will you ever amount to anything.

You can see how my negative definition of "Self" took shape. Your self-image was likely developed in the same way, if not by the same events. You've tried time and again to make changes or improvements, with differing levels of success. That's because entering a new habit into your life, even if it is for the better, is often seen as foreign and is therefore rejected by your V.S.S.

Remember, the purpose of the body's immune system is not to decipher between good and bad. It was designed to recognize "self" from "non-self." Your Viral Success System operates the same way. It sees "self" as your current and longstanding thoughts, habits, processes, ideas procedures, actions, and perceptions.

The good news is, just as your body's immune

system can be treated to allow acceptance of a transplanted organ, your V.S.S. can be treated so the necessary steps towards success will be seen as "self" and defended as such. Your V.S.S. can be trained to recognize a *New You*!

In this book, I will explain my system for going from an ordinary life filled with doubt and uncertainty to an extraordinary life filled with confidence and success. I have proven this system in my own life, over and over again, in several different fields. I share the following not to brag, but to show you what is possible in your own life.

With the help of some great colleagues, I created a patented suture and tying kit to teach surgical knots and stitches that is sold in a medical school bookstore. I filmed a 6-disc DVD series on surgical assisting and I co-authored a surgical assisting textbook all available and sold internationally. I started a surgical staffing company that generated 2.8 million dollars in its first 36 months. And, to top it off, I achieved all of these things without any degree in medicine, nursing, or even business. I achieved a 7th degree black belt in Okinawa Karate and founded two Martial Arts schools; one has been in business for 16 years while the other has been in business for 18 years. Furthermore, I was inducted into the U.S. Martial Arts Hall of Fame in 2005 as Instructor of the Year. Additionally, I am a Certified Life Coach, a Motivational Speaker, and with this book, I am a published author for the third time.

Well, I hope you're starting to see why I believe in this system. These are just some of my life highlights. I've achieved great things in my life, and I know that by using these steps, you can have the same success and more!

# STEP ONE:
## Directing Your Thoughts

*"You cannot become what you need to be by remaining what you are."* — Max de Pree

Can you guess how many times you were told "No" by the time you were age 5? How about at the ages 9, 13, or 18 years old? In your formative years, you're taught to obey the instructions of your parents, family members, and other adults. There were consequences for not doing so! Once you started school, you learned the importance of getting along. Teachers might have made you feel bad, chastised, and even ostracized for unwanted behavior. Conversely, if you followed your friend's requests and desires, you felt liked, accepted, wanted and even appreciated.

**RUBEN:** I easily made friends at school because I was funny and kept other kids laughing and entertained. My issues came when my friends who knew me as Mr. Funny needed a bit of laughter in class. "Do it," they'd say. They wanted me to make some sound, face or gesture that would break the monotony of the lesson. To be honest, I liked the attention. My teachers were somewhat lenient on me because I would help them out as needed and I followed instruction most of the time.

One particular day I had a problem because my friends needed a laugh but my 3rd grade teacher, Mrs. Miller, wasn't in the mood for any of my shenanigans. "Just one more time," one of my best friends, Bradly Perez, asked. Mrs. Miller had already warned me the last time but I made the noise and laughter erupted. Wow! That was the best response that noise had ever gotten.

"Come up here Ruben" Mrs. Miller said without even turning around from the chalk board. She pulled out a slip to send me to the Principal's office. My heart dropped. My parents had a "you better be sick" policy regarding any phone calls from the school and at this moment I became ill. She wrote out the slip and sent me on my way. It was like walking the green mile.

Mr. Giese, the Principal knew my family especially my Grandpa Byrd. My Grandfather was a father of 12 and was no nonsense when it came to school and behavior. I think my mother learned the "you better be sick" policy the hard way from him. Mr. Giese asked me what happened and I told the truth as I knew that was the best thing to do. He laid his paddle on the desk in an act of intimidation and said I will have to call Reverend Byrd. You guessed it; my Grandfather was a preacher as well. He was also the initial contact for the school as my parents were hard to reach at their jobs.

Mr. Giese greeted my Grandpa and then read the slip. After reading it he went on to say; "this doesn't seem like something you would want your grandson doing Reverend Byrd and I just want to know how you want me to handle it." "Paddle him and save some for me," my Grandfather said. I was really sick now. I questioned if I would even be Bradly's friend after this experience.

After the paddle from Mr. Giese, the whipping from my Grandfather, and the whipping from my mother then my father, I decided I would rather lose friends than be a comedian. As a matter of fact, to this day I hardly tell jokes just because of that experience. Well, that's an exaggeration, but that lesson certainly left a lasting imprint on me. I am still more cautious with my sense of humor and very thoughtful as to whom I want upset with me.

We all learned that not rocking the boat was the easiest way to skate by. To get along, you have to go along. Keeping everybody around you happy began to play an important role in your day-to-day lives thus, in this environment, the victim mentality was born. You learned to give up things you wanted to do, say, and be!

These powerful lessons were being stored in your Viral Success System as you developed the concept of "self". Self-doubt is the V.S.S. equivalent of a virus to your cells. A virus causes chronic infection and if untreated, will travel from cell to cell destroying each new healthy cell it encounters until there are no more left. Viruses can remain dormant until just the right opportunity for them to act.

Self-doubt is usually acquired through a

negative interaction or relationship and will lie in wait until the right host appears, then it springs into action. In your V.S.S. these hosts are new ideas, decisions, or changes. It is difficult to be successful or obtain personal satisfaction with prevailing thoughts of fear, self-doubt, worry, blame, jealousy, and lack of purpose. If those negative feelings and emotions are determined by your V.S.S. to be considered as "self," you will then tend to argue for these weaknesses.

When people continually tell you what you can't do, what you will not ever achieve, and how you won't ever amount to anything, it registers in your mind. Because you have internalized these thoughts, they are now considered as "self" and contradicting (positive) statements come under attack by your V.S.S., even if they could set you free from the negative mindset. You refuse to believe in yourself because, for all intent and purposes, you've been programmed against it.

**RUBEN:** "From a young age, I felt I was always being compared to someone. Let me explain. My mother was the 3rd oldest of 12 and her two youngest sisters, Melodene and Veronica, seemed more like my older sisters than my aunts. Melodene, my mom's youngest sister, was and still is as smart as they come and in school she was a straight "A" student. There was never a need to look at her report card because we always knew what it said. I was Melodene's nephew.

Veronica, number 11 of 12, was and still is charismatic, outgoing, funny, and entertaining. Even as a kid she would perform on the spot and make people laugh effortlessly. She was born to be in front of a crowd. I was known as Veronica's nephew. My older brother, Robert Jr., was naturally athletic. He could run faster, jump higher and, as a rule, excel in any sport better than I could. He let me know it and so did everyone else. I was Robert's little brother.

Even well-meaning people - including family - always compared the things I did to the highlight reels of these three family members. I was never as smart as Melodene; never as outgoing as Veronica, and never as athletic as Robert. I heard this so much that after a while I never expected to be any of those things either.

Achieving my success required me to accept that when people made these comparisons, they were trying to give me examples of how outgoing, smart, and athletic I could be if I just tried a bit more. I don't know if they were right or not. I do know there are better ways to encourage someone however, as the saying goes, 'if they knew better, they would do better."

It wasn't until I got around people who didn't know me in the context of my family that I was finally seen as 'Ruben' instead of as 'somebody else's lesser relative'. At that point, I finally took responsibility for creating my own individual identity."

In order to live an extraordinary life you must examine your current thoughts and ideas. Taking responsibility for your actions, ideas, and your lives as a whole is an important part of the success equation. Maybe because you live on your own, have a job, and provide for your family or yourself financially, you believe you've taken responsibility for your life.

However, when it comes to your success, happiness, relationships, or personal satisfaction, you blame others as to why you are not getting what you desire. An "it's them" mentality focuses on what others have done; it's a "victim" mentality. Conversely, successful people often ask the question "what is it that I am doing that is giving me these results?"

Directing your thoughts requires that you get in touch with whatever may be preventing you from reaching your goals. There are many feelings, ideas, worries, and concerns that, however justified, need to be tamed if you are going to unleash the unbelievable power within you. These common emotions keep you from reaching your full potential! Consider which thoughts you may be holding onto and why these thoughts must be changed. I'd like to share some scenarios where my client's negative thoughts were being defended by their V.S.S.

**MARK:** "Erin and I got married in our 20s. We'd been married for 16 years with two children when I realized I never went after my dream. A college degree would help a lot with my earning opportunities, but I felt like it was too late. How was I supposed to go back to school? I needed the overtime at work to support our standard of living. I was more worried about what our family and friends would think if we downsized to a smaller house than I was with a strategic move. But I just kept thinking, "If I wasn't married with children, I could get my degree."

This is a perfect example of using the victim mentality. However, Mark changed his thought process from "this is why I can't do this" to "let me figure out how I can make this happen." This change in thinking allowed him to realize that he could accept the offers for help from family, friends, and especially his wife. He also rationalized that there were plenty of people with families who got their college degrees; and that he did not owe an explanation to anyone as to the decisions he had made to downsize his life. This level of thinking allowed him to completely make over his "self" concept and obtain his degree, as well as ultimately start, run, and successfully manage his own business.

**RITA:** "I worked at my company for 7 years while going to school in the evenings. When I graduated with my degree, I was offered a management position with a different company in another state. Everybody - my coworkers, family, friends, and current boss - they all pressured me to turn it down. They said things like, 'You'll be breaking up the family' and 'We need you here, what would we do without you?' So, I stayed for another year, unhappy and more in debt. I gave up additional income that my current employer wouldn't match."

She blamed her family and coworkers for her negative attitude, financial decline, and for keeping her "trapped" in this situation. Although Rita had always seen herself as responsible, she had never faced a situation like this one. She came to realize that she had put the decisions for her personal success, financial and professional advancement, as well as her goals and dreams under the control of others. She had been following the "people pleaser" mindset which was constantly being defended by her V.S.S.

After participating in coaching, Rita realized that these relationships were not fostering the growth she wanted and desired. However, after she was able to align herself with like-minded individuals, she was able to focus on restructuring her concept of "self" and went on to exceed her initial expectations.

**KATHRYN:** "As a divorced mother, I worked hard and often said, 'Those kids are my life.' When they were little, people always complimented their manners, behavior, and appearance. Then, my middle son started down a wrong road filled with poor decision-making. Subsequently, my happiness, joy, self-confidence, and self-worth all began to spiral downward. I felt responsible for my child's behavior and actions.

It took a major overhauling of my thinking to realize that my son had free will. He chose his behavior and he had to find his own way. I could only offer him help and not worry about what others thought of me as a parent. Putting my goals and dreams on hold wasn't going to change his ways. But, on the other hand, reaching my goals would put me in a better situation if he chose to accept help in the future."

Even with bold statements of faith and compelling reasons to act, you must rewrite the definition of "self" in your V.S.S. At one time or another in your life, you may have conceived a dream or goal, yet quickly talked yourself out of it by thinking about all the reasons why it wouldn't work or why you can't have it.

All of these clients had reasons to put their dreams on hold 'for now' and accept less than they originally wanted, or simply give up and quit. They each had to overcome countless obstacles and setbacks that tested their resolve and determination. And yet with all of that, they were all able to reprogram their definition of "self" and it started with the changing of their thoughts. As one client put it, "I had to get my thoughts, actions, ideas, and mental images all building and supporting the same ideology."

This powerful mental shift reprogrammed my

client's definitions of "self" and shifted their outlook. Without implementing a change in the way they were thinking, they would not have been able to achieve the success they wanted and dreamed about.

They all had made the shift from the "it's them" mentality to the **#ItsOnMeMentality**. They made the decision that if they were going to enjoy a life of sustained happiness, achieve their goals and dreams, and be able to radiate positive energy, it would be their own responsibility. Although they still had feelings of doubt, fear, and at times worry, they did not and do not dwell on them.

The Viral Success System is precisely that – a system of multiple parts, not a single entity. To function well, it requires harmony and balance. However, functioning well does not mean that it is guiding you towards success; it means it is accurately recognizing what has been programmed as "self" and what is being introduced as "non-self." To guarantee success you must redefine your current concept of "self" and let your V.S.S. do its job. On the following page you'll find specific action steps to help you do just that.

# Mastery Tip #1

**#WatchWhatYouSayToYourself.** Without keeping a close eye on your mouth and your mind your words can taint your spirit, drain your energy and create a toxic attitude.

Be mindful of the fact that unmonitored thoughts can turn your faith into doubt, turn your destiny into despair, and eliminate your ability to dream.

Start each day with uplifting thoughts. Consciously direct your mind to focus on the positive. Speak of what you have rather than what you lack. Allow your energy to create universal alignment with others. Accept that it is YOUR TIME TO WIN!

# ACTION ITEMS FOR STEP ONE
## Overcoming Self-Doubt

*"Erase self-doubt by working to build your strengths instead of focusing on your weaknesses."*
— Rodolfo Costa

1: Think about a goal you've wanted to achieve. What 3 thoughts have kept you from achieving this goal?

- _____
- _____
- _____

2: Looking back, where did those thoughts originate from? Write them down.

- _____
- _____
- _____

3: What should your thoughts be in order to achieve this goal?

- _____
- _____

- _____

4: Knowing what you should be thinking, what can you do when these negative thoughts come into your mind?

- _____
- _____
- _____

5: List 3 techniques you currently have for breaking through negative thought patterns.

- _____
   _____
- _____
   _____

6: Who do you turn to when you are having these thoughts of self-doubt?

- _____
   _____
- _____

- _____
 _____
 _____

7: What resources available at www.destinationmastery.com can help you overcome these thoughts?

- _____
 _____
- _____
 _____
- _____
 _____

# STEP TWO:
## Acting With Gratitude & Faith

*"Faith is believing in what you do not see and the result of that faith is seeing what you believe."*— Saint Augustine

Wouldn't it be great if the things we wanted in life came with a guarantee? Well, the good news is, they do. The difficult news for many of us is that we are the guarantor. What we do, how we act, and how committed we are to what we want will determine what we will receive from this journey called life. Moments of fear and periods of uncertainty are an inevitable part of the growth and development process. Furthermore, we must learn to be thankful for what we already have in order to receive more. In this chapter I will illustrate how planting the seeds of faith and gratitude are key components to your V.S.S.

When I was learning martial arts I was taught that the students should always bow to the instructor. However I realized that as an instructor I should have just as much gratitude and appreciation for my student as they had for me. We should be bowing to each other. There could be no student-instructor relationship if either party was missing. My goal was to establish long-term meaningful relationships with the students as well as with their families.

**RUBEN:** My best friend, Kevin, and I had been teaching martial arts for years and now we finally have our own building for a martial arts school. I'd been in the building before, but this would be the first time walking in as a 50/50 owner. This place was once a grocery store; a ceramic shop; as well as a vacant building but, now, just a disaster. The building had plumbing, electrical, and insulation issues. Actually the list of needed work was extensive and well beyond our abilities to fix and financial resources at the time. Kevin told me how the owner came down on the price because he knew us and thought it was a worthwhile undertaking.

Kevin was enthusiastic and excited. But I remember standing in the middle of the main room with a smile on my face, thinking to myself, 'What a disaster!' Now, you are probably wondering; 'Then why did you agree to buy it if you couldn't see how it was going to work?" Well, that is what you do in a collaborative, achievement driven, and supportive relationship. Based on our history of working together, I trusted Kevin's judgment. This was a "faith" situation and I believed it would pay off." I was thankful to have a building to work on and believe it or not, being thankful goes a long way.

University of California at Davis, Professor Robert Emmons discovered some very interesting and eye opening results from his research on gratitude and thankfulness. Professor Emmons found that people who kept gratitude journals on a weekly basis reported fewer physical symptoms, exercised more regularly, felt better about their lives as a whole, and were more optimistic about the upcoming week compared to those who recorded hassles or neutral life events. In addition, participants who kept gratitude journals were more likely to make progress towards their personal life goals.

The findings in this study confirmed what I came to believe about gratitude. The findings speak to the physical and personal benefits of gratitude. This is why in order to have a strong Viral Success System, gratitude is a must. I personally keep a gratitude journal. The one I use is actually a phone app. I have it set to popup in my phone screen twice per day. The first time is in the morning so that I can start my day with the things I am grateful for. The second time is in the evening so that I can record the experiences and encounters from the day. By keeping my mind on what I am thankful for, I direct my thoughts towards positivity and abundance which gives me the ability to attract more of the same.

**RUBEN:** Dr. Martin Luther King, Jr. said, "Faith is taking the first step when you can't see the whole staircase". That was exactly the case in our situation and I was overwhelmed with the thought of the project. One deliberate step was all I could focus on. I had no idea how Kevin and I would get this building ready, but I knew of the saying, "Start where you are at, use what you have, and do what you can." I was committed to this process.

First order of business was removing all the clutter and we let everyone know what we were doing.

I liked this because it was something I could do. As a matter of fact, this was one of the first of many lessons I learned by working on this project. *Focus on what you can do and allow the universe to provide the rest. Here is what I mean by that.

Imagine being in your car at a stop light and across from you, there is a guy with his door open trying to push and steer his car at the same time. You realize he had run out of gas. As you watch you realize that in spite of his best efforts he is making very little headway. Then out of nowhere, someone jumps out of their car and starts pushing his. The car starts to move. Then another person joins in and before you know it there is plenty of pushing help and the driver is inside steering. You realize that the universe came to his rescue because he took action.

I was truly blown away by how many people were willing to help us clean up, especially since pizza was our only real currency. Many of our current students and their parents would make arrangements to help us on a particular weekend. We always let them know how much we appreciated them and their willingness to help. A sincere "thank you" was always a sufficient payment; the pizza was an added bonus.

You have no doubt heard the principles of karma and it seems that everyone has heard the sayings "you reap what you sow" and "what goes around comes around". Take it from me, this project proved it again and again. Your life will manifest from the universe what you have firmly planted, not necessarily what you are currently planting. In other words, you can't get the harvest until the seeds have been planted and have had time to develop and grow. These individuals' willingness to help was just that, a willingness to help. Their lives had been impacted by us in such a way, that even though we were charging them for classes throughout the week, they showed up to help us for free on the weekends.

Here is another confirmed lesson from the project; **#ImpactDrivesIncome**. If you have a product or service, don't set out to make money; be thankful that you have the opportunity to make a positive impact. Focus on how what you do will enriches or enhances your customers or client's efforts or experiences. How does your product or service make their life or job easier? If you don't run a business but are looking for ways to make a difference with your life, find a way to serve others. My favorite book says "the greatest among you shall be your servant".

I remember thinking, "how are we ever going to get this all done? We don't have the tools and there are a lot of things that need to be done that we just simply don't know how to do."

The Universe came to our rescue with help from Kevin's dad, Ken Wilson. Mr. Wilson was a supervisor at a plant by trade and had skills, knowledge, and talent just waiting to be shared with us. He voluntarily came to help us weekend after weekend – in fact, he always seemed just as excited about the project as we were. He showed us things like plumbing and basic electrical work, carpentry and drywall. But the real lesson we came to see through his dedication and commitment to helping us was how being willing to serve makes a greater impact.

Mr. Wilson was grateful for the opportunity to help us and we were grateful for his help. One Friday night he told us that he wouldn't be able to help us on Saturday because he needed to go in to work. I realized that each weekend he had spent with us, helping us, teaching us, and inspiring us, he could have been at work making money or simply enjoying his weekend. After all, he had worked all week. But it wasn't about the money for him. It was about showing up for his son and me.

He was planting seeds. His sincere desire to help meant more to him than making the extra money or just relaxing. And because Mr. Wilson was respected by his friends and work colleagues, many of them with particular high dollar skills like electrical work, came to help us for no charge. They did it simply as a favor to Ken.

This story is an example of how gratitude and faith are powerfully interwoven within the Viral Success System. By Mr. Wilson planting seeds of gratitude and service we were able to get a discount on the building from his neighbor of over 20 years and get free help and consultation from very skilled professionals. By Kevin and I truly caring for the families in our program, the students as well as their parents showed up to help weekend after weekend on a project that took over a year.

At the very start of this project I had no idea how we were going to do it. Looking back now, I can't imagine anything that could have kept us from doing it. Everything you have completed in your life to this point started with the first step. By you taking deliberate steps to practice gratitude and faith, you are strengthening your V.S.S. and planting seeds of prosperity for the future. Take the first step and accept help from the universe.

## Mastery Tip #2

Regardless of your current situation or circumstance **#LetYourFaithSpeakForYou**. Rest assured, life will throw you curve balls, sometimes just to test you. Things like relationship troubles, sickness and pain, as well as financial and transportation challenges are all par for the course. **#LetYourFaithSpeakForYou**.

In spite of what you may be going through right now, this too shall pass. It may seem as if it is one thing after another with no end in sight. **#LetYourFaithSpeakForYou**. However, there is a POWER within you that is STRONGER than any obstacle you face. You may be down but YOU ARE NOT OUT!

If it gets to the point where you can't even talk, **#LetYourFaithSpeakForYou**.

# ACTION ITEMS FOR STEP TWO
## Increasing Gratitude & Faith

*"Faith is spiritualized imagination."*
— Henry Ward Beecher

1. Living with faith mandates that we let go of some of the things that have kept us tied to our old ways. What do you need to let go of in order to live with faith?

   - _____
     _____

   - _____
     _____

2. How would your life be different if you relied more on your faith (in projects, in decisions you make, in choices you take or don't take) as you move you towards your goals?

   - _____
     _____

   - _____
     _____

3. Gratitude requires us to change our way of thinking from a place of negativity or the "glass half empty" mindset to one of positivity, or "glass half full" mindset. This sometimes means recording our thoughts. Write down 2 things that you are truly grateful for.

- _____
  _____

- _____
  _____

4. What system do you currently have in place to record your daily gratitude?

- _____
  _____

- _____
  _____

5. How will living from a place of gratitude change your daily living? How will it affect your mindset?

- _____
  _____

- _____
  _____

6. We all know that in order to be able to harvest a crop, there first had to be a seed planted. Faith is planting the seed, believing that it will grow. As you think about desired outcomes, what new seeds (habits of faith) do you need to plant?

- _____
  _____
- _____
  _____

7. What resources available at www.destinationmastery.com can help you increase your faith?

- _____
  _____
- _____
  _____

# STEP THREE:
## Choosing the Right Associations

*"When a dove begins to associate with crows its feathers remain white, but its heart grows black."*
— German proverb

Collectivity, the cells within the body work together in a spirit of cooperation to keep the body running. The body's immune system serves as the protector of this intricate arrangement.

Your many relationships are the cells of your life working together to keep you functioning. The importance of meaningful relationships rooted in a deep sense of mutual respect and cooperation can't be stressed enough. Your relationships can catapult you to new heights or keep you stagnant as you contemplate your lack of progress.

Your V.S.S. not only watches over what is considered to be "self", it also works to accept and reject relationships with those that you encounter. Therefore, if your V.S.S. is not programmed for success, it will draw you towards negative relationships and reject the very connections that could move you in the direction you want to go with your life.

**JAMES:** "I grew up in the inner city with a group of kids from the neighborhood. We were all within a few years in age and lived within a 5 square block radius. Same school; same playground. I can't remember a time when we weren't together and we always had each other's back! These friends would have died for me - we did almost everything together.

I joined the Army Reserves, separating me from my running buddies for a few years but, when I got back, it was like we never missed a beat. There was one thing that was different now though. Now I had goals and dreams. These aspirations marked a difference between the fellas and me. The guys seemed to be doing the same things we did when we were teenagers. It was as if life stood still for them, and simply froze them in time, but who was I to judge?"

His time spent with his childhood friends had programmed his V.S.S. in a way he wasn't even aware of. When he started working in Kansas, he met some people who were like him "but different." They had things like "mission statements" and "relationship contracts." James had never heard of such things, but he knew they were business owners and that was something he wanted to be a part of. An agreement was finally struck, making him part owner in a new venture.

**JAMES:** "Initially, it was difficult for me to adjust to these new relationships. I came to realize my mindset was composed of doubt and lack of trust, but not until after a year into the business relationship. As the time went on, my consciousness level grew to new heights, and I gained valuable insight as a result of these relationships."

James's story is a perfect illustration of the mental shift that takes place when you are developing your V.S.S. Removing certain people from your life is going to be a difficult task. However, realize that your happiness is worth more than a toxic relationship. On a physical level, removing unwanted viruses from your body makes perfect sense. You should want to do the same thing on a mental level.

***JAMES:*** "After I'd been gone for several years, I went home to visit family and friends. Now my life is different; I'm a husband and father. But when I ran into my old friends, in an instant I was one of the guys again. They were headed out for a quick run, and I jumped in the car so we could catch up. Before I knew what was going on, though, the car stopped and my friends got out to confront a guy for some reason or another.

I tried to get their attention to defuse the situation, but punches flew and things got ugly. In an instant, I realized I was no longer cut out for this. I had changed and what used to seem routine was now absurd. I swore that, if I made it out of this situation, I was never hanging out with them again."

One of James's business associates, Kevin, suggested all of the owners start reading the same books and then discussing them. This would allow everyone in the business to speak a common language. Every month, each owner would be responsible for recommending a book for everyone to read, and add to their personal library. The books would be purchased with company funds and for those who spent a significant amount of time in the car; they could choose the audio version.

*JAMES:* "I would have refused to participate in anything I thought was a "book club" that's for sure! Initially, I thought everyone would suggest books that had to do specifically with business development or marketing. But that wasn't the case. Typically, the books that were recommended dealt with personal growth and success. Kevin wasn't just a talker; he was a doer. He led by example. Really, he was using this as a way to elevate our individual and collective consciousness. When we got together to talk about the things in the books, he always suggested how to implement those things into your daily lives and schedules."

There was no room for doubt that James's V.S.S. was undergoing a dramatic transformation. Collectively, the partnership served as a support system focusing on the things they wanted to accomplish, developments they wanted to see in themselves and in each other, and all the while developing their ability to pass on what they were learning. The individuals involved in the business partnership have become some of James's most significant connections. Not only are they the type of relationships that are off the charts in terms of probability for success, but they are also conducted effortlessly. These relationships represent sincerity and the utmost of respect. They provide the necessary resources, support, and self-confidence to attain goals and desires.

For my clients, eliminating negative and toxic relationships were absolutely necessary as they committed themselves to redefining "self" in an effort to achieve personal success.

**ERIC:** "You will always encounter naysayers when trying to achieve goals, move ahead, or develop yourself. I group those individuals into three categories:

1. Pessimists. Those whom are envious of anyone who attempts to leave the

"nest", often due to their own insecurities.

2. True Haters. Those individuals who are downright jealous of your God-given gifts and are unwilling to recognize, enhance, or maximize their own inherent talents.

3. Gate Keepers. Individuals whom, via innuendo, omission, or dismissal, do not want you to enter their "circle" due to social or political reasons.

Teamwork is key. At each turn in my journey, I've tried to learn from and be willing to pass wisdom to anyone who shared advice to me that lined up with the Word of God. You don't have to become close, intimate friends, but when the "bell" tolls, one must put aside personal views, attitudes, and preconceived notions in order to reach common goals.

In this next example, they served as an energy drain on each other, and anyone that spent any significant time around them. Lori, a participant that was interviewed for her weight loss success was able to lose 120 pounds and has kept it off for 5 years.

**LORI:** "My relationships with negative people contributed to my weight loss failures time after time. It wasn't until I really listened to what was being said that I really understood just how negative my circle of friends really was. We all had things we didn't like about ourselves and it was like we couldn't wait to share them with each other. If anyone said something positive, it was almost like an unconscious contest to see who would be the first to undermine it. For instance, if I said, "I'm thinking of going back to school," someone would then say, "Why? I know people out there with degrees that can't even find a job. What classes would you take anyway? Don't you think you are smart enough already?" After a while, I would join in and say, "What was I thinking?"

Understand the current state of your V.S.S. may make it difficult to realize what needs to be done and may reject your taking action all together. Like in Lori's situation, you may have been in these relationships for so long they seem normal to your V.S.S. Relationships that are favorably oriented towards your success provide you with a sense of self-confidence, increased self-worth, and inspire you to trust in your abilities. You should be able to communicate worries, concerns, and other issues without being belittled, put down, or made to feel incompetent.

Tell people in your circle of friends that you are looking to make changes in certain areas of your life. Are they supportive of you improving and moving ahead? Keep one thing in mind; just because they ask questions, doesn't mean they are not supportive. Really get a feel for their mindset. Ask them about their future plans for progress or advancement. Take note of their answers. Maybe the relationship needs time, space, or needs to be ended.

Once you have identified that a change is needed in a relationship, be prepared to act. If possible, let family and close friends know you will be spending your time in a different way. You're not changing their behavior, so be honest and keep the focus on you. If you can't have the necessary conversation in person, do it over the phone or in an email. The important thing is that it gets done.

I would bet no matter what it is you would like to accomplish, there are some elements of imitation that you can employ to jumpstart your progress. Here are some questions to ask yourself as you imitate your way to success.

- What is the status of your current relationship?
- What does the financial picture for your life look like?
- What is your current health status?
- How do you feel about your current employment?
- What about your current network of friends and associates?
- Are you satisfied with your current level of education?
- Is your spiritual life where you want it to be?
- Are you giving attention to your goals,

dreams, and aspirations?

- Do you have a system to regularly evaluate these areas of your life?

- How is your relationship with your children or your parents?

- What activities are you involved in that gives your life meaning?

These are but a few questions you can ask yourself to get clarification of your current state of "self." Regardless of the answers, you have the ability and responsibility to make adjustments as necessary.

Remember, no one makes you feel sad, mad, or ruins your day - **#YouPermitItOrYouPromoteIt**. Negative feelings arise but you must learn to let those emotions pass quickly as you reprogram your V.S.S. If you can't break away from the negative people completely, set boundaries and avoid being drawn into negative conversations. More than likely, they aren't going to change their disposition towards you especially for you to grow. However, you can change how you let it affect you and your path to personal growth.

There are many clever sayings about how the people you associate with affect you, such as: 'You are the sum total of the six people you hang around most' or 'Your network determines your net worth.' I was amazed by a comment offered by one of my clients. She said, "Foster those relationships that bring you closer to your true happiness, and in doing so, you will have created your Dream Team that will take you to your ultimate championship of life."

The bottom line is your V.S.S. requires you to take action in the reprogramming process. By simply starting this process, you are empowering yourself to move in the right direction. Eliminating the negative people from your life takes courage, and can prove challenging at times, but it pays dividends, and you will reap the rewards.

# Mastery Tip #3

**#ChooseYourAssociationsWisely.** There are some people who have ALWAYS been negative and they will ALWAYS be negative; *avoid them.* These emotional leeches find the worst in even the best of situations and make it a point to share their findings. Their greatest strength is pulling others down so stay away.

You have the POWER and the RESPONSIBILITY to keep your associations positive. Choose people that you can *share with* and *gain from.* Don't waste time trying to alter the behavior of someone stuck in a permanent funk! Some people stay that way to repel positive, upbeat and thankful people.

Remember, you can't change the people around you; however you can change the people you are around. **#ChooseYourAssociationsWisely.**

# ACTION ITEMS FOR STEP THREE
## Creating Your Dream Team

*"Isn't it kind of silly to think that tearing someone else down builds you up?"* — Sean Covey

1. Write down 1 major goal you have in each of the following areas of your life: Personal, Health, Wealth, Spiritual, Business and Professional.

   - _____
   - _____

2. Write down the six people/friends you spend the most time around. Come up with six names to put down. Don't say, "I don't have six".

   - _____
   - _____

3. Being brutally honest, can the six people listed

in questions #2 help you achieve the goals you listed in question #1? If no, why not?

- _____
  _____
- _____
  _____

4. Is there anyone that you need to add to your circle to help you achieve your goals? List their names or titles (ex. trainer, financial advisor) in the space below.

- _____
  _____
- _____
  _____

5. List specific things you want these individuals to help you with.

- _____
  _____
- _____
  _____

6. Do you have people currently in your circle to help you with these things? If so, list them here.

- _____
  _____

- _____
  _____

7. How can a Destination Mastery coach aid you as a member of your team?

- _____
  _____

- _____
  _____

# STEP FOUR:
## Sacrificing for What Is Necessary

*"Be miserable. Or motivate yourself. Whatever has to be done, it's always your choice."* — Wayne Dyer

Think about the goals that you want to accomplish. It might be to get a raise at your current employment or start a business. You might have some physical exercise goal that you want to achieve. It may be something creative like writing a book, recording an album, or crafting an art project. You may have a desire to start or improve a relationship. How about heading an opportunity for a charity or creating an after-school program.

How long have you wanted to reach your goals? How many times have you tried to get there? If you look back, you may see obstacles that seemed larger than you could handle. That's because, as previously stated, the changes you want to make are not yet part of your 'Self'. However, keep in mind that you have the ability and responsibility to develop, mold, and shape the self that it will be continuously defending and protecting.

Remember from the Introduction, stasis is the most important process that takes place in your body. In our everyday lives, we don't use the word stasis; we say things like structure and stability. Using these terms doesn't mean the situation is at its best, but rather that it is operating in a way that will continue on as is. Think about it. Most habits — be they judged good or bad— are stable and involve structure. The important fact to recognize here is that in order to get what we want from life we are going to have to change our old habits and ways of thinking and this will require us to get out of our comfort zone.

Whatever it is that you would like to achieve is going to require you to do something different. Remember, doing the same thing will only get you the same results. Doing something different means change. Change most often means growth. You might have to change the way you think, or take on new ways of responding to challenges, or obtain additional training or knowledge. Whatever the case, you have to take action.

You must be willing to sacrifice what's

comfortable for what's necessary. It's not going be easy, but it's going to be worth it.

Rosetta, who was one of the individuals interviewed for this book overcame daily difficulties in her workplace.

**ROSETTA**: "I worked for a company that was dominated by men. It was in the mid-seventies when I started there and jobs were hard to come by. I made it my purpose to do my best and always keep a positive attitude. However, the prevailing attitude of the workplace was that women were inferior. That made it difficult to be positive at times. However we always have the option to direct our thinking towards something positive."

Routinely Rosetta would be asked to train new men that started with the company. She would do as she was asked however it bothered her to watch the men she trained be promoted to leadership and higher paying positions while she was kept at the same level.

***ROSETTA:*** "Everything was fine until I asked about being promoted. That set off a litany of negative events directed towards me as well as other women in the department. These activities discourage many of the female workers there and some actually quit their jobs. I was amazed that women were actually insisting that I stop inquiring about advancement and fair treatment."

Rosetta's sense of "self" was well developed. Her faith was strong and her beliefs conveyed a strong sense of justice. While her superiors and co-workers could make things difficult for her; they could not make her take on a negative attitude or actions. She challenged the system and filed a discrimination law suit which she won. She stayed with the company for over 25 years earning the respect of her peers, superiors, and subordinates and earning equality for the women in the company

***ROSETTA:*** "It was a very difficult time but it was a victory for equality. Instead of trying to change the way others react, you have to change the way you react to others. You must be willing to sacrifice certain relationships and comforts if you are going to change you situation.

*JAMES:* "I gave up my old friends, the ones I ran with for most of my life. But, once I became a husband and a father, my life took on a whole new meaning. My responsibility to guide and provide for my family gave me the drive to change and I have never looked back."

*ROSETTA:* "Many people criticized me for filing - and winning - the gender discrimination lawsuit against my employer. Some made threats and some retaliated in various ways. I was an outcast for a period of time. But filing the suit was something I had to do. I had to do it for myself, for the women who came before me, as well as those who would work there in the future."

*LORI:* "My feet hurt, my back hurt, and my hips hurt. I was falling apart at the age of 28. It clicked for me one day after someone asked if my weight would limit what I could do with my kids once they were older. My weight affected my health and my relationships. I made up in my mind that I was not going to miss out on the activities with my children! I knew at that moment that I would do whatever it took to lose the weight."

**ALEX:** "I'd been in and out of rehab, but I was finally able to stop using drugs once I made a complete mental shift. I saw what the drugs were doing to me, my family, and those who loved me. I remember being shocked to see a picture of myself, looking as if I'd aged by 5 years. I made up in my mind to make the change. The last time wasn't different; I was different. I wanted to live a full life."

One of the most important factors in getting what you want is the "why" that drives you, the reason you want better or more out of life. You must have a "why" so strong it will allow you to bounce back time after time. As one speaker put it, 'You must have a purpose larger than any problem that you will face.'

If you are going to go from ordinary to extraordinary you must have a compelling reason to carry you through your doubts and fears. Every successful person, including myself, had a powerful reason as to why they pursued a particular goal or dream.

Your ability to change, grow, and develop is going to be critical and crucial to your newfound goals and desires. Therefore, you are going to have to have reasons that will keep you focused and committed. You have to commit to the commitment. Again, often times when you fail, it's because you didn't have a strong enough commitment; you didn't have a large enough "why".

Take some time to write out the reasons why this new achievement is important to you; why you must have this new goal. How it is going to change your life? In what ways? How are you going to feel when you succeed? How will it change your environment? How will you perceive yourself after you achieve your goal? Your 'Why' will keep you focused on developing your ideal 'Self.' Once your V.S.S. begins defending your new definition of 'Self', your 'Why' will keep guiding you towards the success you're looking for.

If you understand the V.S.S. up to this point, then you understand that it will defend whatever you make it believe is true about you. If you're uncertain and you believe the obstacles are greater than what you are trying to achieve, your V.S.S. will reinforce that thought. If however, in your mind, you've programmed a reason that will compel you to act- regardless of the circumstances - it will keep you headed in the direction of success. Let go of uncertainty and believe that you have to win, to succeed, and to accomplish. Do that and your V.S.S. will only accept things in line with that mindset.

Confucius said, "By three methods you may learn wisdom: First, by reflection, which is noblest; second, by imitation, which is easiest; and third by experience, which is the bitterest." In his book, *Change Or Die*, Alan Deutschman discusses the three steps to lasting change. He refers to them as the three R's: Relate, Repeat, and Reframe.

Deutschman suggests that when you form and maintain emotionally connected relationships with new individuals, those new relationships provide a level of believability that change is possible, regardless of how hopeless it once seemed or how many past efforts to change have failed. Lasting hope and encouragement can be inspired by others once you decide to reprogram your V.S.S. You can literally change your reality by modeling new ways to think about situations, circumstances, and life in general. Through repetition, these new skill sets will become automatic and second nature forming new behavioral habits. Here is a breakdown of the concept.

- Relate - An individual forms and maintains new emotionally connecting relationships with new individuals such as, teachers, organizations, mentors, groups, and/or communities that promote and inspires lasting hope and encouragement. The relationship(s) provide(s) a level of believability that change is possible regardless of how hopeless it once seemed or how many times efforts to change have failed in the past. The individual learns new strategies, methods, and techniques that are being taught and shared through the new relationship(s). As a result of the new connection(s), he/she is sold on the idea that change is possible.

• Repeat - While involved in the new relationships the person will learn new patterns of behavior that will be practiced and mastered. Through repetition these new skill sets will become automatic and second nature forming new behavioral habits.

• Reframe – He/She literally changes their reality providing new ways to think about situations, circumstances, and life in general. This new way of thinking would have been impossible before.

As you look at the areas of your life that you want to change, select a model to pattern it after. How do you know which model to select? Well, it's simple. Find someone who is already getting the results that you want and use their strategy. Why? If you do the same thing you should get the same results. It isn't necessary to figure it out for yourself all the time. If you find someone you trust, who can give advice, guidance, direction, or a level of success you can model after, then you can start taking action while you gain more knowledge.

**RUBEN:** "The day my ex-wife, Jennifer, called me on the phone, crying, was very unusual and it alarmed me. We have two children, Monica and Spencer, who both live with her and her new husband.

"Did something happen to Monica?" I asked nervously. 'No.' she said as her voice quivered. 'Did something happen to Spencer?' This was my natural next question, to which she replied, 'No.' My next question to her was, 'Is something wrong with you?' Again, she said no. Since the issue did not involve my first three questions the possible problem was too vast to guess.

Still crying, she explained that she'd spoken with the kids' swim coach. Both Monica and Spencer competed in swim meets and I made it a point to attend whenever I could. "The swim coach pointed out how differently Spencer conducts himself when you're around", Jennifer said, "I've also heard this from his teachers and I've even observed this myself."

'Okay...' I replied, still not understanding why this would be anything to cry over. 'You are a great dad and I think he could learn and grow into a great young man if he lived with you.' Then I understood why she was crying.

I've come to realize that most of the time a decision isn't tough because we don't know what to do. It's tough because we don't have the courage to do what we know and not what we feel."

These are all stories of sacrifice. Look at it this way; if what you were doing was enough to get you where you wanted to go, you would already be there.

Remember, if you want to change something, you have to change something. Understand that everything you want has associated costs. You'll have to give up certain behaviors in order to get what you want. It's these associated sacrifices that often keep you from having what you actually want. For instance, if you want to be a successful entrepreneur, you may have to give up being timid or disorganized. If you want to become more productive, you will have to give up procrastination and lateness. You can't be effective and excuse oriented at the same time. For this reason, your 'Why' has to be so strong that it propels you forward. Your purpose must force you to give up being who you used to be, in an effort to **#BecomeWhoYoureAbleToBe**.

In the end you have two choices; be prepared to sacrifice for what you want, or stay the same whether you want to or not. Sacrificing for change on a small scale now will help you to develop the resilience to go after change on a larger scale as you continue to grow.

# Mastery Tip #4

**#GoAfterWhatYouWant.** Stop expecting life to just hand you what you want. It's not that type of party. Sure, you see other people with nice homes, jobs, relationships and more. What you don't know is what they have gone through to get the things you see. Here is what I know; in life, things have a cost and a price. **#GoAfterWhatYouWant**.

Know that you can have whatever you want but you must be ready and willing to sacrifice for it. You've heard the old saying, no pain, and no gain. Well that applies to you as well. Stand your ground! Face your fears! Commit to paying the price for the success you desire! I'm not saying it will be easy. I'm saying it will be worth it! **#GoAfterWhatYouWant*!*

# ACTION ITEMS FOR STEP FOUR
## Sacrificing For Success

*"Great achievement is usually born of great sacrifice, and is never the result of selfishness."* — Napoleon Hill.

1. Look back at your answer on Action Step #1 in the last section. List those same goals here.

   - _____
   - _____
   - _____

2. Have you tried to accomplish any of these goals before? If "yes", what was the outcome? If "no" what makes them a priority now?

   - _____
   - _____
   - _____

3. If you want to change something you have to change something. List the things you will need to change about yourself in order to achieve these goals?

    - _____
      _____
    - _____
      _____
    - _____
      _____

4. Growth requires sacrifice. List the things will you have to sacrifice in order to achieve these goals (friendships, habits, thoughts).

    - _____
      _____
    - _____
      _____
    - _____
      _____

5. List the challenges you foresee in being able to make these sacrifices?

- _____
   _____

- _____
   _____

- _____
   _____

6. How can the people on your "Dream Team" list help you overcome these challenges?

- _____
   _____

- _____
   _____

- _____
   _____

7. Looking at the expected challenges, how can a Destination Mastery team member help you gain

clarity and direction?

- _____
  _____

- _____
  _____

- _____
  _____

# STEP FIVE
## Embracing the Idea of Failure

*"I have not failed, not once. I have discovered several thousand things that will not work."* — Thomas A. Edison

Be ready fail your way to success. Wait, what? That's a contradiction in words and actions. How can I possibly expect to turn a failure into a success? Excellent question!

Failing or the fear of failure might actually discourage you to the point that you can't move forward. So if, to avoid embarrassment, you simply never take any chances, you ensure that you'll never have to face failure. But, at the same time, you will remain stagnant and never grow. Your goals, dreams and your road to success all come to a screeching halt.

One of the greatest things about kids is that they do not go into new situations with the fear of failure. A child's V.S.S. hasn't been tainted with life's negativity yet. They go into a new situation without a preconceived notion of what the outcome will be. Instead, they allow themselves to try something first, allow themselves to fail, learn from their mistakes and move on.

Let's look at an everyday situation. As a young child, you first rode your tricycle triumphantly up and down the block. You were getting pretty good at riding it too! Pretty soon, though, you started to outgrow your beloved tricycle. The seat didn't fit quite right, and your knees were just about hitting the handlebars. But that new two-wheeled bike looked so big and wobbly, and you weren't sure you could handle it...

So what was the answer? Give up before you began because the fear of failure was so strong? Never try again and always fear learning something new? No, even back then at an early age, your V.S.S. was engaged, and you were ready to move on and experience something new!

With that two-wheeled bike, it was all a matter of balance. Did you tumble or fail along the way? Of course, you did. The difference is that you picked yourself up, brushed yourself off, and started all over again. That was the key lesson each of us learned as we wobbled this way and that, or took a tumble. You eventually learned that if you sit straight with your weight in the middle, and don't lean too much one way or the other but just balanced in the middle, you could actually ride!

Your childhood V.S.S. was programmed to overcome obstacles and challenges. So what is it that is holding you back now? What changed in your V.S.S.? What keeps you from the success you are currently seeking?

One of the most unfortunate things about failing is that people get very discouraged by it, instead of being challenged to try again. In fact, some people get so discouraged about failing, that the fear of repeated failure is all they concentrate on. The valuable lesson that could have learned and later on applied is totally lost. What's worse is what replaces it.

*ALEX:* "I had a pretty normal childhood and my parents are still married. If anything, they were a little overbearing and protective of me. I was never too outwardly social – only had a couple friends at any given time. I was a little shy; I kept to myself and was quiet. I tried drugs for the first time the summer after sophomore year of high school. I got high not just by the drugs but also the atmosphere around it. I got high on the acceptance. Acceptance was a big part of my using. I now realize it was a self-confidence issue.

I got caught and was kicked out of a youth group. My mom went ballistic. She grounded me, took away my driving privileges and sent me to rehab right then and there. She made me see a therapist and I hated that. I didn't think I needed to be there. I spent 3 months in rehab. I knew that I didn't want to do drugs anymore, but as soon as I got out, the first thing I did was look up my old friends and got high. I was stoned 6 hours out of rehab."

Unfortunately, Alex's V.S.S. fell victim to the self-destructive activity virus. The fact that Alex went right back to the same negative activities shows that his V.S.S. did not have the necessary immunity to resist these negative viruses. Drugs became a cycle of repetition in Alex's life that went on for several years. His V.S.S. continued to see the chemically altered state of mind as 'Self.'

**ALEX:** "As I look back, I realize my many failures to quit using were due to the fact that each time I wanted to be sober, the drugs were everywhere, even in rehab. One day I tried a different approach and it worked! I was finally able to stop after I made a complete mental shift. I stopped hanging with those friends who were using drugs. I stopped going to the places where I knew drugs would be accessible. I stopped giving myself excuses that allowed me to wander back into a relapse. I got counseling and listened to my sponsor. I refused to worry about my past mistakes. I simply failed my way to success!"

'Fail' is a harsh-sounding word that has negative thoughts and feelings attached to it. At first glance, it would appear to be on the virtual other end of the spectrum, as far removed from success as possible. However, there's incredible value in discussing this because failure brings with it a learning experience.

Failure can be viewed as trying something, and

not getting the result you wanted. Or setting goals but somewhere along the way, something happened, and you fell short of what you have imagined. So what do you do when this happens? You could stop trying all together. You could train your mind to believe you can't do something because it didn't work out the last time. Or challenge yourself to go the extra step. Look beyond the supposed failure, and examine why it failed. There is always insight to be gained and analyzed. Failure will actually strengthen your V.S.S.

**RAPHAEL:** "I believed sports could definitely get me to college on a scholarship and maybe even further. In an effort to introduce myself I traveled to tournaments across the country for 3-5 days at a time to play in front of various coaches. All expenses had to be paid for by my single mother, family, friends, or anyone who was 'down for the cause.' I focused on practicing my skills over the tournament weekend so that one day I could make a team that had a sponsor.

In the spring of my junior year of high school it happened. I finally signed with a school in Louisiana. But, about a week and a half before I was to leave, the assistant coach called to tell me that my scholarship papers weren't sent back in time. Also, they just got a new athletic director who wasn't going to honor them due to budget cuts. I was livid! But then I chose to ramp up my work ethic to an all-time high. I went to a local junior college, practiced with the team and took classes.

Quitting or giving up was not an option for me. After being there and doing my best I was recruited by a school in Texas. It wasn't in my original plans but it worked out great. I was able to start and my senior year; we won our division conference and played in the NCAA tournament. It was an awesome experience and I was able to complete my 4 year college degree on a basketball scholarship."

**#PlansFailPeopleQuit.** Have you ever considered that perhaps people don't fail as often as they think they do? Instead, they merely quit too soon. Most people stopped at the 'I can't do this' negative thinking. All possibilities stopped. All chances for success were taken away because, both consciously as well as subconsciously, a roadblock was put in your way and it was standing between you and success.

**RUBEN:** I remember watching the Oprah Winfrey show where she introduced 'The Secret'. I was very intrigued by the ideas that were being discussed; so much so that I decided to try it for myself. I created my vision board as suggested on the show. I had always wanted to be a public speaker. I loved the idea of being able to inspire a crowd.

The blue board had pictures of famous speakers in a circle with my picture in the middle. I had even cut out pictures of crowds and affixed them to the board. I put the board on the wall in a very visual place where I could see it all the time. Even with all of this there was one problem. I wasn't doing it to prove the theory right; I was doing it to prove the theory wrong. I really didn't believe I could do it and belief was a major part of the "Secret".

I remember standing in front of the board saying 'I'm not smart enough to speak. Who would want to listen to me?' There was an internal battle in my head going on at all times which consisted of what I wanted to happen and what I believed could happen. My V.S.S. was protecting the wrong "self" and doing a good job of it. The fear of failure got the best of me and I blamed it on the Secret not being real. 'I knew this wouldn't work!' I said as I took the poster down and threw it behind the couch.

How many times are you going to give up and let failure, or the fear of failure stand in your way? When you give up prematurely you have written your destiny. You have created your own failure because you stopped trying. You simply gave up too soon. Furthermore, you trained your V.S.S. to recognize that giving up is a part of "self."

**RUBEN:** It had been quite a few years since I had made the speaking vision board and I was standing in my kitchen. I had just written some notes for a surgical procedure I was going to assist on the next day. I walked away and then returned to read what I had just written.

'Man, I'm smart!' I said aloud.

'What?' my wife responded.

'I'm smart!' I said again looking her in the eyes. 'I know you are smart; you married me!" She replied.

We both laughed. I was experiencing a genuine **#BreakthroughMoment**. It was almost like I was having an out of body experience while I was reading what I had just written. In that moment, I felt invincible.

'If I am smart, it means I can speak.' I announced as she looked at me in a somewhat bewildered way. 'I am going to call Les Brown." I said confidently.

'Les Brown the Emmy winner, voted Top 5 Speakers in the world, inducted into the Speakers Hall of Fame Les Brown? She questioned.

'Absolutely!' I replied. Something had changed. I acted with a new level of faith. I looked up his information on the internet. I was not able to speak to him but I did get his direct email.

I sent an email that day and he called me the very next day. He said he was inspired by my message and was looking forward to working together. I started training with him and joined his Platinum Speaker Program. To date, he has called me several times to speak at engagements with him.

The whole time I wanted to speak I was being limited by the thoughts in my head. I was 6 inches from success. What does 6 inches from success mean? You ask. It's the space between our ears. The deciding factor of my success this time was that I immediately took action. Keep in mind that doubt reduces action but **#ActionReducesDoubt.** The saying, 'Nothing ventured, nothing gained', has never been more on target than when developing a positive V.S.S.

That doesn't mean to put yourself into a dangerous situation, like leaping off a building or spending your last dime on a long shot just to prove a point or stare down a fear. It means, realize that fear is very powerful but you have control over it. Fear is a choice. You can either spend your life hiding and running from it, or you can accept it as part of life. What you do with it, or about it, will sculpt the meaning and result of the experience.

Are you ready to be successful, truly successful? If so, then you must be ready to learn from your mistakes or failures, and not be consumed by them. The bottom line is that life is an on-going road of trials and tribulations, failures and successes. You are in a constant state of growing, striving and reaching for success. As one client put it, "I simply learned what I could from the previous trial and then moved in the new direction."

Another client said, "Instead of focusing on the things that went wrong, find the ones that went right and build from there." Do not let your fear of failure keep you from reaching your goal, and striving for success. You need to make yourself a promise. You can try and fail, but you can never quit. NEVER QUIT!

# Mastery Tip #5

**#DontStopTrying**. You have to *expect to be tested by life*. Rest assured that in life you will face setback after setback. There will be times when the issue is financial. There will be moments when your challenge is emotional. There will be situations where your problem is physical. *You will win if you don't stop trying.*

You have bounce back power! There is a strength within you that is greater than any obstacle you face! **#DontStopTrying**! Whether you have gotten off track, side tracked, or even had to back track *don't stop trying*. Your success is just on the other side of a setback. **#DontStopTrying**!

# ACTION ITEMS FOR STEP FIVE
## Overcoming Setbacks

*"A setback is a just set up for a comeback."*
*– Dr. Willie Jolley*

1: List 3 goals that you have wanted to achieve but stopped due to setbacks or obstacles.

- _____
- _____
- _____

2: What were the setbacks or obstacles?

- _____
- _____
- _____

3: What parts of the plan went well?

- _____

- _____
  _____
- _____
  _____

4: What lessons did you learn from your previous attempts?

- _____
  _____
- _____
  _____
- _____
  _____

5: How can you use the lessons you learned from your previous attempt to make your next attempt successful?

- _____
  _____
- _____
  _____

- _____
  _____

6: Many companies bring in consultants to help them get an outside perspective. How could having an outside perspective benefit you?

- _____

- _____
  _____

- _____
  _____

7: Which Destination Mastery Coach would benefit you and why?

- _____
  _____

- _____
  _____

- _____
  _____

# STEP SIX
## Having the Will to Succeed

*"When one's mind is made up, this diminishes fear; knowing what must be done does away with fear."*
— Rosa Parks

Think of how many times in your life you've encountered change. Change can be a frightening experience for many. It means a departure from everything you currently know and are comfortable with. When our immune system is weak or compromised we cannot handle exposure the various environments just as many people cannot handle change, and do not adapt very well because of their underdeveloped Viral Success System. But not you!

A common problem is that many people treat personal growth and development as 'optional' and so few people ever take the time to actively and deliberately improve themselves. But not you! You realize that developing a strong Viral Success System is arguably one of the most important things you can do with your time. It can easily be argued that your very purpose for being here is to maximize your true potential.

Because you now have a renewed sense of self-confidence made possible because of your healthy V.S.S., you have learned that a failure does not mean that you have failed. It simply means that you may need to re-evaluate your plan of action, and alter it so that you can achieve the success you are looking for. Fear has been removed and you're ready to take on this challenge with a positive outlook. Your path to success is wide open.

**RUBEN:** In 1990 as our country was facing off with Saddam Hussein, I was a 20 year old sergeant in the 410th Evacuation Hospital out of Topeka, Kansas. It was clear to me that our unit was going to be activated in support of Operation Desert Shield/Storm and that I would be going to war.

I was not scared of actually going to war as my youth and naiveté prevented me from seeing the real danger. My main concern was if I should challenge the promotion board and attempt to become one of the youngest Staff Sergeants our unit had ever had. I knew there would be additional responsibilities but having a higher rank would eliminate me from doing some of the less desirable things as well as increase my pay.

'What did I have to lose?' I asked one of my fellow soldiers. 'What if you don't get it?' he asked me in return. That was a good question. The worst thing that could happen was that I would not pass the promotion board; however, I would gain valuable insight as to how the process worked. The bottom line was, I was going to war. What I had to decide was if it was going to be as an E5 or E6. I decided I would take the challenge.

I did fine on the written exam and the oral portion solidified my promotion. I marched into this new life experience with a new found level of confidence. All it took was the will to do it.

One of the greatest revelations on your road to self-discovery should be understanding the difference between a choice and a decision. Notice, if you will, the two very strong but different words used here: "choice" and "decision". It is imperative to your success that you understand the meaning of these two words and how they relate to your V.S.S. For the purpose of understanding, we will classify a choice as selecting between options that have very little effect on the outcome. Making a choice would be like deciding between using salt and seasoning salt. This choice simply comes down to personal preference.

On the other hand, a decision is made with conscious effort taking into consideration the ramification of the outcome. When we think in terms of things like cheating or stealing, we base those concepts on our beliefs and/or core values. We make a decision not to steal or cheat. Making a decision is taking personal ownership for how things should come out. It is through the decision making process that you own your results.

Treating a major decision like a simple choice often leads to states of confusion and uncertainty where the decision maker states "I don't know how I got here".

By simply understanding the difference between a choice and a decision and giving the decision making process the consideration and respect it deserves, you can alter the direction of your life.

Hopefully you've made the decision to leave behind and walk away from all the things that were holding you back. You now decide what actions to take in your life, which paths to follow, which receptors you will respond to, and which plans you intend to press into action. This bold and empowering move enables you to stop being a victim of circumstances, past mistakes or problems. It puts your focus on what is happening now, where you stand today, and just as importantly, in the direction you're going.

So where does choice enter into the picture? Choice refers to filling in the details once the major decisions have been made. Because you're taking the time to understand the difference between decisions and choices you will have a new way to give yourself a clear set of instructions.

Your mindset can be viewed as literally setting switches in your mind, and then depending on what you have these switches set to, they can alter and effect what happens to you in your life. Your sustained thought patterns determine your mindset; your mindset determines what you see as "Self." Once that determination is made, your V.S.S. goes into action protecting and defending those determinations just as your body's immune system defends the cells that carry the distinctive "Self" marker molecules. If your mindset is switched to "positive" you can expect to have positive life experiences. I once heard a quote that said, "Consistently act the way you want to be and soon you will be the way you act".

One of my clients epitomizes this mindset and constantly radiates positive energy. He is a MD of anesthesiology and during the time the interviews for this book were being completed, he served as the Medical Director for a facility in central Illinois. If you asked him why he is so positive at work, he will tell you that he is doing what he was 'called' to do. Even though he faced setbacks, obstacles, and hurdles, he managed to keep focusing forward. As he told me,

"Once I made the decision to become a physician, no one other than God could have thwarted me."

**ERIC:** "My faith does not allow me to harbor or maintain a spirit of fear. Brief interludes of fear, anxiety, or negative thoughts cannot be avoided; however, it is what one does with those negative feelings or emotions that count."

Building a complete Viral Success System will serve you well and allow you to stay positive even in difficult times and circumstances. By understanding the whole picture, your positive mindset results in a positive attitude, and because of your healthy V.S.S. system, you've learned many of the necessary skills you need to succeed. Not to mention, you attract others who share your ideals of success along the way. All of this was made possible because of the decisions you made, and how you set your internal switches.

**RUBEN:** It was shortly after my divorce and I was operating on auto-pilot. My switches were set to under achievement. I knew I wanted more, but the will was lacking. Fortunately, one of the nurses at the hospital where I was contracted saw something in me. Her name was Edwina Blackman. She asked me to come to her office to speak one day.

While in her office, she talked about my positive qualities, my positive attitude and her belief that I could do far more than I was currently doing. In the back of my mind, I believed her; however I still had questions and doubts because of the failed marriage. Fortunately, she would not give up. Every chance she got, she gave me small bits of encouragement. I came to realize that my situation was just that - a situation - it did not define me, and she could see something that most people couldn't see, and I believed she was right.

I stopped feeling sorry for myself and started appreciating the fact that I had the opportunity to start all over again. Yes, I would be working to start certain parts of my life all over again and yes it would be difficult but I was willing to put in the work. I would be operating the command and control switches.

When you create an environment within your V.S.S., one where positive thoughts and actions prevail, your V.S.S. is on autopilot, and is in a constant search mode for positive reinforcement to sustain itself. You have trained your mind to extract the positive from each situation you encounter. This allows you to meet any challenge head on, without the fear of possible failure. Your V.S.S. is strong, and you have learned yet another valuable lesson. This lesson is adaptability, and it will serve you well.

This positive mindset has set the stage for a positive attitude, and your positive attitude is infectious even to negative thinkers! Even the most negative thinking individuals will be more than a little bit curious why are you so happy all the time? Is life treating you better than everyone else? Why are you always so successful at the many different things you try? You can wear your smile with pride because you truly are happier as a person, and you have learned how to achieve what you have set out to do. Just think how empowering that alone can be!

*RUBEN*: In 2001 I was in Wichita, Kansas working as a surgical technologist. Myself along with three other individuals had an idea; we would introduce the concept of surgical first assisting to the facility we were contracted. The difference for me would be, instead of handing the instruments to the surgeon, I would take the place of his or her partner and assist in the surgery freeing up the partner to do more pressing things. Most everyone did not think this would be possible because this had never been done before at these facilities in this way nor was there licensure for this profession in the state of Kansas.

I knew it would be an uphill battle however I had nothing to lose and the world to gain. The first thing I did was speak to the surgeons informing them of how this would allow them to maximize their time. Next was the administration. I met with Lowell Johnson, hospital V.P. and provided him with information on how other facilities in other states were making this work. Surprisingly, he thought it was a great idea.

>"We will let you do it under one condition" he said.
>"What's that?" I replied.

"We are not going to pay you for it." He said.

This was not exactly what I had in mind but you know the old saying, "A career is something you love so much you are willing to do it for free; but you do it so well they are willing to pay you for it." If we were going to be paid we would have to sell them on our service. We were going to make an impact and that would drive our income.

We decided to move our paid shifts to 3pm to 11pm and assist as needed for free from 7am to 3pm. Needless to say most of the staff thought we were crazy for working for free. They did not have our vision. I know that sometimes **#FreeWorkIsTheKeyWork**.

The days were long and the temptations to stop were many. In spite of the fact that we had no guarantees we were committed to staying the course. The internal commitment was a key component because outwardly it seemed as if we weren't making progress. We were however planting seeds of success and tending to them regularly.

As it turns out, the surgeons that we were helping on a regular basis told the administration that they would bring all of their cases to that facility if they could get our help. In turn, the facility offered us $100,000.00 each to work there and provide the service. There is something to be said for going back at it again and again!

Develop your own success quote (a lesson in the will to succeed). "Success is not measured in the results of the attempt but rather in the willingness to attempt the results." This means that on some level, once you decide to pursue success you have already succeeded.

Confusing? Let's think about it for a moment. Before you picked up this book you had no idea of its contents and how it would impact you. Now you find yourself contemplating how to change your mind, your habits, your friends, and even the way you function. Why? Well, because the real you has been illuminated. It may have been hidden away and oppressed by any one or maybe even any number of the reasons discussed in the previous chapters of this book. No matter, it is awake now.

Even with those reasons screaming at you trying to drown out the words as you read them, you kept reading. Finally, someone is writing the words that somewhere deep inside you always knew to be true about yourself. Yeah, you have had friends to commiserate about your situation with, and reasons not to try but even then deep down you didn't believe what they were saying and to with what you were agreeing was the truth about the real you.

Now you have a reason to change your focus, your path, your approach, and ultimately your life and nothing, or no one is going to deter you. That is in effect what the quote means. You always knew there was something more for you, now you are determined to make it happen. You are already a little more successful just for thinking this thought.

A powerful quote can make an impact that is why every chapter in this book is prefaced with one.

Successful people make those quotes often just in speaking normally. They never intended any one sentence to be a standalone quote. Someone else sees the power of the words they spoke and uses them to inspire others and themselves. You don't ever see a professional quote writer. You only see successful people making statements that turn into powerful quotes.

Now that you have embraced the will to succeed, you are already a successful person. It is time for you to start thinking about how your words may be in italics in a future book inspiring others. You have used words to hold yourself back all this time, (either the ones you utter yourself or the words of others). These are quotes also. Think about it, you continually used them to keep yourself where you were. You have already written quotes for your unsuccessful self. Now you are going to use your own words to move yourself forward.

Think of yourself where you want to eventually be in your pursuit of your own successes. What will that you say to the person you are right now? What will that you say to others who have similar success goals as you the ones you have achieved? You are going to become that person, so somewhere inside you already know what you will be saying when you get there! As powerful as quotes from others are, they are not yours. You are your own person, and who better to inspire you now than the person that you are on track to being!

# Mastery Tip #6

**#KeepSwinging**. Life is a fight for territory and we have to *keep swinging.* One way or another, life hits us all. Every day someone gets the news that they have cancer, diabetes, high blood pressure, or some other illness. Every week holds the news that a job was lost, a relationship ended, or someone was a victim of crime. **#KeepSwinging**

You may have to face financial issues, transportation setbacks, even the loss of a loved one. In life you will get hit. You will get hurt. You might even get knocked down. But in the words of Muhammad Ali, "the canvas is no place for a champion". Stand up, grit your teeth, and **#KeepSwinging!**

# ACTION ITEMS FOR STEP SIX
## Making Decisions and Choices

*"The will to win, the desire to succeed, the urge to reach your full potential... these are the keys that will unlock the door to personal excellence."  - Confucius*

1: Having the will to succeed comes down to a reason 'why'. What are your reasons why you must be successful?

- _____
- _____
- _____

2. Why are you passionate about these reasons?

- _____
- _____
- _____

3: When faced with an obstacle or setback, what about these reasons would make you want to fight through it?

- _____
  _____
- _____
  _____
- _____
  _____

4: What are some things that you need to take control of that you may not have felt like you could control in the past?

- _____
  _____
- _____
  _____
- _____
  _____

5: How will understanding the difference between choices and decisions change your view on achieving your goals?

- _____
- _____
- _____

6: Can you identify any choices you made in the past that should have been treated with the thought and seriousness of a decision?

- _____
- _____
- _____

7: Looking at the different coaches on the www.destinationmastery.com website, who would you like to connect with to get help making those decisions?

- _____
- _____

# STEP SEVEN:
## Redefining Your Authentic Self

*"The brave don't live forever but the cautious don't live at all. The only thing that's truly terrifying is the unlived life."* — Bill See

It is often the regrets we have about our lives that overwhelm our thoughts and prevent us from moving forward and reaching our goals. Regret for the decisions we may have made or didn't make, the relationship lost, the interview we never went to; all of these things weigh heavily on our minds and can keep us set in our way of thinking. This mindset forms our V.S.S., then when any new way of thinking comes up, we simply dismiss it as "foreign" and push it out of the way.

Overcoming the regrets we still hold close to us allows our V.S.S. to become re-programmed to positive thoughts, releasing of old habits, and embrace the idea of new thinking. But simply overcoming regret is not enough. We must avoid future regrets by truly pursuing the things that give our lives meaning.

Since you have a choice, why not set the standard high and get the maximum satisfaction out of your life? After all, you won't get a second chance at life. What is to be gained by living a life of mediocrity? Why accept the ordinary when you can easily program your life for the extraordinary?

Your body's immune system works relentlessly to defend and protect you regardless of how well you take care of it. How ironic that the better care you take of your body, the stronger your immune system's ability to defend you. Since your V.S.S. will work hard to defend your actions, beliefs, and ideas, it only makes sense to program your "self" with a definition worth defending. By having a strong sense of "self" you gain the confidence to live authentically.

**RUBEN:** My original degree is a Bachelor of Science in Criminal Justice with emphasis on juvenile corrections. I remember doing my internship at the County Youth Detention Center in Topeka, Kansas. I recall walking up to the brick building for the first time as I looked at the tall fence designed to keep the kids in. "I would hate to live in there" I thought. I guess no one liked living there however because of choices they had made, many kids spent time there.

After my first week I had the system down. I recognized all the keys and was aware of the scheduled activities. I studied the policy manual to gain a deeper understanding of the profession. Even with all of this something was missing. This wasn't shaping up to be what I was expecting. In my mind I was to be leading and mentoring young kids that may have been somewhat misguided. My days here mostly consisted of saying 'stop that, sit down, line up, and go to your room' over and over again. Honestly, I was just babysitting and I questioned why I needed a college degree to do so. My sister was 11 and she had babysitting jobs too. I had to figure out what my next step was going to be. I knew that I wanted be a mentor to youth but there had to be a better way.

"Karate school" I thought to myself. I had been studying martial arts and this would be perfect for what I wanted to do. As great as this sounded in that instant, I immediately started to question how I could possibly own a school. All the responsibilities of marketing and advertising bothered me. What if I wasn't good enough or experienced enough? What if I could not compete with all the other established schools around town? Anyway, what did I know about being a business owner?

I spent day after day trying to talk myself out of the idea but something kept calling me. Then, I started to focus on what I had as opposed to what I lacked. The more I thought about it I realized I had the most important ingredient. I had the "why". I would do it for the kids. Willis Whitney said "some men have thousands of reasons why they cannot do what they want to, when all they need is one reason why they can."

There are many reasons why you must live authentically and avoiding regret is the main one. Looking back now, after being inducted into the U.S. Martial Arts Hall of Fame, teaching students of all ages, as well as training champion martial artists, I realize that my success was always in my hands. In spite of all the people that told me I couldn't, I still did. I can't imagine living with the regret of "what if" simply because I did not try. Sydney Harris hit the nail on the head when he said "Regret for the things we have done can be tempered with time. It is regret for the things we have not done that is inconsolable."

Your life can be partitioned into different areas. By analyzing what shows up in those areas, you gain an understanding of the reality you've set for your life. If you're getting happiness, success, and progress, it's because that's the reality you chose to create. If areas of your life have hit a plateau or become stagnant, likely you have accepted that state for now. Regardless of the current situation, the good news is, you have the power to change it.

Much like an actor that you see in multiple movies and roles, performing masterfully as different characters, you have the ability to rewrite the script in every area of your life.

Whatever you have accepted for yourself in any area is currently being protected by your V.S.S. If you have set the standards high, it will settle for nothing less. If you set the standards low, it will accept nothing more. Simply put, you can accept what's currently showing up or rewrite the script.

When an actor performs a new role, he gets the script which has been created with detail, allowing the actor to bring it to life. All the while the director watches with a keen eye for what is showing up versus what was written in the script. Because the director knows exactly what is supposed to show up, he can intervene at any time to make corrections or adjustments. You are the director of your life.

It's your responsibility to write the script and act the parts. And, because you know what is supposed to be showing up, you have the ability to make adjustments and corrections at will. Your goal should be a script worth defending and creating a life worth living. As General George S. Patton stated, '**#LiveForSomethingRatherThanDieForNothing**.'

Failure is a necessary option. I often hear people talk about how they regret making a decision because they feel like it ended in failure. The people with the most regrets in life are those that are afraid to fail. Nothing is achieved without failure at some point along the road. Therefore if you're only going to take the easy road and try to avoid failure then you're setting yourself up for a life of regrets. The people who are successful in living their lives with no regrets are the ones that fall down 9 times and get up 10. There is simply no other way to get what you want.

No doubt you've heard that the definition of insanity is doing the same thing over and over again and expecting different results. Well, if that's the case, then the definition of sanity must be doing the same thing and expecting the same results. Use this modeling definition to your advantage and to move yourself forward. As you look at the areas of your life that you want to change, select a model to pattern it after.

How do you know which model to select? Well, it's simple. Find someone who is already getting the results that you want and use their strategy. Why? If you do the same thing you should get the same results. It isn't necessary to figure it out for yourself all the time. If you find someone you trust, who can give advice, guidance, direction, or a level of success you can model after, then you can start taking action while you gain more knowledge.

I have seen so many people waiting to get all the answers before they take action. Then, because they could not get all the answers, they never took action.

You have seen and know individuals who have gone on to accomplish great things. You know couples who have great relationships. You know people who really seem to get things done. Yet, often times you don't even bother to ask how they have gained the level of accomplishment or achievement that they have managed to manifest in their life. By simply asking, you may get the insight that you need. You could ask them for suggestions on books to read, audio courses to listen to, or events or seminars to attend. More than likely, they would give you a recommendation.

Furthermore, there is a whole host of books on any subject that you would want to look up in the areas of success, life, health, diets, workouts, spirituality, and many more! The problem for most people is they, like I once did, invest in "shelf" development and not "self" development. They buy the book and put it on the shelf and often times, not even reading it before tucking it away for good. If we all did the things that we heard and read, we would all be skinny, healthy, and happy. However, many times this information is taken as just that...good information. In order to create a life worth defending, you have to put these plans into action.

# Mastery Tip #7

**#BeYourself**. The world will try to get you to conform. You will get pressure from all sides and every direction urging you to relinquish your authenticity. You will be told what you *should* and *shouldn't* do. You will be told what you *can* and *can't* be. *Be yourself*. Don't mistake other people's opinions for facts.

Hold firm to your commitment to be YOU! Take a stand and challenge any feelings of self-doubt or regret that creeps into your mind. You are here *on purpose, with a purpose, and for a purpose*. Refuse to believe anyone that tells you otherwise. You were born an original. DON'T DIE A CARBON COPY! **#BeYourself**.

# ACTION ITEMS FOR STEP SEVEN
## Living without Regrets

*"As you grow older, you'll find the only things you regret are the things you didn't do."* – Zachary Scott

1. Living with regret can keep us trapped in a mindset of constant failure and frustration. What are some of the things in your life that you regret?

    - _____

    - _____
      _____

2. What do you feel caused you to feel regret? (Bad decisions/choices, associations, mindset...)

    - _____
      _____

    - _____
      _____

3. Taking responsibility allows us to begin to move forward. Do you assume any responsibility for

these feelings of regret?

- _____
  _____
- _____
  _____

4. What can you show gratitude towards now to avoid regret at a later date?

- _____
  _____
- _____
  _____

5. How can you enjoy this process of change? How will doing this affect you and the end results?

- _____
  _____
- _____
  _____

6. Many regrets come from not even trying something. What are some things that you need to try now so that you don't regret not trying them later?

- _____
  _____
- _____
  _____

7. Staying on task is key to avoiding feelings of regret. How can you use a Destination Mastery coach to help you stay on task?

- _____
  _____
- _____
  _____

# CONCLUSION
## Working With Mentors and Coaches

*"Listen and learn. Or don't listen, and learn the hard way."* -Ruben West

You have a plan, the next step is to put it to use by taking action. You must employ these new thoughts as "self". Stick to your plan and ask for help if you need it. In fact, encouragement is good even if you think you can go it alone. You will be all the more successful if you have a Success Dream Team around you!

Coaching is an effective process used to support individuals in creating something new for themselves. I work side by side with my clients coaching them by providing perspective and support for self-knowledge as they accomplish their business and personal goals.

I personally help people implement the 7 steps to viral success and achieve balance and cultivate the tools necessary for them to evolve into a life filled with happiness and serenity. I believe everyone has the tools they need inside to lead a more fulfilling life. I simply guide them along an empowering path that will awaken these tools, focus on their passion and ultimately lead them to a more fulfilled self. If you are ready to find your way to a more balanced you, then coaching is just the thing for you.

Even the best athletes look to their coaches and mentors for guidance and improvement on their work and their progress. They realize that they don't need to rely strictly on themselves to grow, learn, and get better – that is why they have a coach; to see things they can't see. Coaches help their athletes (or clients) to see the whole picture and get clarity about what it is that they want out of the end results.

**RUBEN:** My most memorable coach was my high school wrestling coach named Jerry Meier. He was what I would call a no-nonsense coach. As a matter of fact I often thought he mistook wrestling for cross-country running. He believed in conditioning and mastering the fundamentals. He ran drills over and over and over and it never seemed as if he cared what you thought about it.

Most sports today don't seem to be as effective as wrestling was under Coach Meier. He was building more than great wrestlers; he was building great people. He set rules that everyone had to follow no matter what a person's skills were. He wasn't easier on you if you were a winning team member nor was he less demanding if you were not on varsity.

It seems that some coaches today want to make every child feel good as oppose to requiring them to push themselves to achieve things beyond that which is easy. Coach Meier knew that, win, lose, or draw, true achievement, true self-worth, and true self-esteem comes from being able to know that you have given your all; that you have pushed yourself to your limits. He never made it easier. He encouraged you to be better. If you were able to do a technique he would say "great now practice it over and over". If you were not able to do a technique he would say, "Keep practicing until you can".

Following Coach Meier's instructions allowed me to learn a technique. Not following his instructions allowed me to learn a life lesson in consequences. I created the opening quote in his honor. "**#ListenAndLearn** or don't listen and learn the hard way". To this day I still have the letter he wrote me on the school's letterhead my senior year. The letter had expectations of me. He expected me to do my best in everything I did and to remember where the wrestling room was.

Coaches act as your accountability partners in all areas of your life. There are many benefits to having a Life Coach and here are just a few. Coaches help you to:
- Design life intentions that include both your business and personal goals.
- Make meaningful personal changes that reduce stress and simplify your life.
- Free up energy and other resources to attract what you want for your life now.
- Enhance the quality of your communication and relationships
- Work through a career or life transition
- Achieve better work/life balance
- Gain clarity, focus and direction

Coaching is also for those successful and growing entrepreneurs, who just need a neutral sounding board to give you straight-up honest feedback and on-going support. There really is nothing like coaching. The best way to learn about it is to experience it for yourself! You have nothing to lose and the world to gain!

# ACTION ITEMS FOR CONCLUSION

What is it that I actually want?

- Weight loss
- Better relationship
- Increased financial success
- Start a business
- Retire
- _____
  _____
- _____
  _____
- _____
  _____

Who is getting these results right now?

- Friend
- Family member
- Colleague
- Co-worker
- Celebrity

- Fellow church member
- _____
  _____
- _____
  _____
- _____
  _____

How can I connect with this person, group and/or organization?

- Set up a meeting
- Place a call
- Reach out via email
- Reach out via social media
- Schedule an appointment
- _____
  _____
- _____
  _____
- _____
  _____

How can I surround myself by or immerse myself in the knowledge of this person, group and/or organization?

- Attend local meetings and/or functions
- Read their book or literature
- Participate in team calls
- Remotely attend online webinars
- Attend live meet-up groups
- Attend regional and national meetings and/or functions
- Be coached/mentored/trained by this person or a member of the group
- _____
- _____
- _____

What limiting beliefs do I have about myself that this person, group and/or organization do not have?

- I can't be successful because of my background.
- I can't be successful because of my past.
- I can't be successful because of my social status.
- I can't be successful because of my education level.
- I want it but I am not cut out for it.
- This process will take too long.
- This will be too painful.
- I don't know how.
- _____
- _____
- _____

Is there a specific plan that you can follow to duplicate their success?

- Is there a written formula or strategy you can use?

- Is there a steps to success program you can follow?
- Is there a guide book you can follow?
- Can a plan be created by you with the help of the person or group member?

- _____
- _____
- _____

What steps can I model or imitate as I start to redefine myself and my success?

- _____
- _____
- _____

- _____
  _____
- _____
  _____
- _____
  _____

What statements or affirmations can I use to program my mind while I undergo this transformation?

- _____
  _____
- _____
  _____
- _____
  _____
- _____
  _____

What techniques can I use to stay motivated throughout this process?

- Affirmations

- Positive reading
- Coaching
- Teamwork
- Success chart
- _____
- _____
- _____

How long do I stay in this process?
- Until I manifest the results I want.
- Until I achieve my goal.
- Until I win.
- _____
- _____
- _____

_____

What Destination Mastery coach can coach me through this change process?

- _____
  _____
- _____
  _____
- _____
  _____

# AFTERWORD

I believe that the universe gives us all ideas and opportunities that can change our lives. Think about the last time you had a great idea or concept and you thought to yourself, "that would be great!" However time passed and you did not take action. Then 6 months, 12 months, even 2 years later you see the very idea you had as an actual product, service, or maybe even an end result of someone that took action. "I thought of that!" you say to yourself. Well maybe so but you don't get rewarded for what you think of.

**#ItsNotWhatYouThinkofItsWhatYouAct On**. You've heard the saying action speaks louder than words. Well, it is time for that action. By implementing these 7 steps your success can go viral and you can live a life that others only dream of.

> *"Your time is limited, so don't waste it living someone else's life. Don't be trapped by dogma - which is living with the results of other people's thinking. Don't let the noise of others' opinions drown out your own inner voice. And most important, have the courage to follow your heart and intuition."*
> *- Steve Jobs*

## About the Author

Ruben was born in Topeka, Kansas. He is currently a 7th degree Black Belt and was inducted into the US Martial Arts Hall of Fame as "Instructor of the Year" in 2005. He co-founded two martial arts schools, both of which are still in business after 16 years. Ruben is a decorated combat veteran serving in the U. S. Army as a Staff Sergeant in Operation Desert Shield/Storm with the 410 Evacuation Hospital.

Ruben is the founder of "The Viral Success System", a Professional Certified Success Coach, Trainer, Entrepreneur, published author, and dynamic speaker. He teaches and trains students and clients all over the world to step into their vision and as he puts it, "Live Your BEST Life".

## Connect with me!

I know that everyone say this, but I really do want to hear from you.

Reach out to me at my website

www.RubenWest360.com

Get social with me on Facebook

www.fb.com/RubenWestSpeaks

Get help and resources at

www.DestinationMastery.com